ANTHROPOLOGICAL PAPERS
MUSEUM OF ANTHROPOLOGY, UNIVERSITY OF MICHIGAN

No. 2

Social Singing Among the Mapuche

by

MISCHA TITIEV

ANN ARBOR
UNIVERSITY OF MICHIGAN PRESS
1949

© 1949 by the Regents of the University of Michigan
The Museum of Anthropology
All rights reserved

ISBN (print): 978-1-949098-41-9
ISBN (ebook): 978-1-951519-65-0

Browse all of our books at
sites.lsa.umich.edu/archaeology-books.

Order our books from the University of Michigan
Press at www.press.umich.edu.

For permissions, questions, or manuscript queries,
contact Museum publications by email at umma-pubs@umich.edu or visit the Museum website at
lsa.umich.edu/ummaa.

CONTENTS

Introduction 1

Sociocultural Background 2

Assembly Songs 4

Conclusion 16

SOCIAL SINGING AMONG THE MAPUCHE[1]

This article is based on material that was gathered in the course of a field trip to Chile from mid-February to mid-August, 1948. The trip was made possible by the combination of a sabbatical leave from the University of Michigan and a generous grant from the Board of Governors of the Horace H. Rackham School of Graduate Studies, to whom grateful acknowledgment is made.

INTRODUCTION

Over the years since 1629, when the "happy captive," Francisco Núñez de Pineda y Bascuñan, first noted that his captors were much given to song, numerous examples of Mapuche singing have been reported and published.[2] Since the contents of the songs are usually packed with meaning, they are properly classed together with such other aspects of oral literature as proverbs, riddles, folk tales, genealogical accounts, and historical recitals. Skill in oratory and associated arts was once a fundamental prerequisite for chieftainship, and even today verbal ability is much esteemed.

To achieve success in this regard is no simple matter, for the Mapuche employ a highly figurative style, full of nuances and subtle turns of expression. Then, too, as Guevara has pointed out, they like to use phrases that are markedly elliptical and laconic, with very few words serving to suggest complete thoughts.[3] Moreover, most of the references that are sprinkled throughout the oral literature derive so much of their significance from close familiarity with Mapuche culture, that outsiders are apt to find them meaningless or enigmatic.

---

[1] For practical purposes the terms Mapuche and Araucanian are interchangeable. They may be applied either to the aboriginal language that was widespread in central Chile before the conquest, or to the natives who speak that tongue. At present the main body of Araucanian speakers resides between the Bio Bio River and Chiloe Island. In their own language Mapuche means "people of the land."

[2] Convenient bibliographic references to these works are given in Donald D. Brand, "A Brief History of Araucanian Studies," N. Mex. Anthropol., XXII (1941), 29 et passim.

[3] Tomás Guevara S., Folklore araucano (Santiago, 1911), pp. 9-10.

The term for a song is ül, and the verb "to sing" is ülkantun. As a rule, the songs have neither fixed numbers of syllables nor regularly determined verse lengths. Instead, they get their effects from a combination of clever wording and rhythmic phrasing in conformity with the patterns of Araucanian speech. If a particular passage is well received, it may be repeated at the option of the singer.

Mapuche songs cover a wide range of topics, including prayers and supplications for supernatural aid, love and courtship, lonesomeness, sorrow, grief resulting from bereavement, enforced separation, poverty, or failure to have offspring. Some classes of songs are rendered by special personages such as chiefs or medicine women,[4] and others are sung in conjunction with the performance of particular activities.[5] Both of these types may be rendered in traditionally fixed forms and are generally accompanied by musical instruments.[6]

A great number of unaccompanied songs are improvised at public gatherings by men or women who take advantage of these occasions to "blow off steam," or to call general attention to some matter of personal concern to the singer. Songs of this kind are called "assembly songs," and their moods may vary from naïve and joyful to slanderous, bitter, or ironic.

Not many "assembly songs" have been published, and scarcely any have been analyzed in terms of their social and cultural meanings. It is the purpose of this paper to call attention to this interesting but little known aspect of Araucanian culture, by providing examples of representative texts, translations, and interpretations.

SOCIOCULTURAL BACKGROUND

During recent decades the Mapuche have been living in a large number of districts or reservations, known in Spanish as reducciónes. Each of these communities comprises a varying

[4] Best known in this category are machi ül, sung by female shamans or machis, in conjunction with curing rites or public ceremonies.

[5] For example, songs designed to bring victory in hockey games are known as paliwe ül ("hockey game song") and are sung before a match begins.

[6] The most commonly used instruments are listed and described in John M. Cooper, "The Araucanians," Handbook of South American Indians, ed. Julian H. Steward (Washington: Smithsonian Institution, 1946), 2, 738.

number of households whose male occupants are, as a rule, patrilineally related. Postmarital residence is patrilocal, and most marriages are exogamic with respect to the husband's reducción. Unilocal residence formerly prevailed, since married sons continued to live under their father's roof;[7] but the modern tendency, at least in the region north of the Cautin River, has been for sons at marriage to build independent houses (rucas) on their natal reservations.

Araucanian communities are characterized by an absence of physical cohesion. There are no streets, no central plaza, no stores or public buildings, in short, nothing that suggests the spatial arrangement of a village or town.[8] Correspondingly, it is not surprising that there should be a minimum of community enterprises. Weather permitting, a fair amount of visiting takes place among friends and relatives who live on the same reserve, but inter-reducción contacts are comparatively few. This is particularly true during the cold and rainy months of winter, when roads wash out and travel becomes all but impossible. For several months of each year, therefore, every community tends to be cut off from its neighbors.

The virtual isolation that prevails in winter is relieved in the spring and fall when intergroup gatherings known as kawin or trawin are held. Members of a given reservation act as hosts, and guests are invited from other districts. Various motives may serve to bring about these meetings. They may be held for the purpose of reaching policy decisions that affect all the participants, to announce important events or news items, to honor a person returning from Argentina or some other distant place, to celebrate a holiday, to hold a thanksgiving ritual or a housewarming fiesta, or simply for the sake of friendship and sociability.[9] Whatever their particular aims

[7] For a discussion of the significance of unilocal residence, see M. Titiev, "The Influence of Common Residence on the Unilateral Classification of Kindred," Amer. Anthropol., XLV (1943), 511-30.

[8] The limits of each reducción are defined by legal title to a given piece of land. These titles were originally allotted to recognized chiefs, who assigned particular portions to their descendants and followers. The collapse of the old system of chieftainship has resulted in much confusion with respect to land holdings.

[9] Public assemblies may be called kawin or trawin. These words are variously spelled by Spanish writers, and some authors try to distinguish between them on the basis of function. All assemblies, however, share so many features that it seems permissible to treat them together. On this point compare Eulojio Robles R., "Costumbres i

may be, all such assemblies are welcome events that provide opportunities for friendly conversation, courtship, gossip, and the exchange of news. Regardless of special functions, too, these events always include in the schedule of activities, feasting, drinking, oratory, and singing.

It is on such occasions that some of the celebrants, generally under the stimulus of drink, may give vent to their inner feelings by improvising songs.[10] The effects of these improvisations are not necessarily slight or temporary. They may lead to the correction of abuses, or they may serve a totally different purpose, for auditors sometimes memorize the songs that strike their fancy and later repeat them from time to time at home. Children are thus given an opportunity to become acquainted with various compositions, which their elders encourage them to learn to sing. The Mapuche recognize that this is an educational technique, and informants point out that it enables youngsters to acquire skill in singing at the same time that it gives them an awareness of the subtleties of their native tongue and an insight into the customs and traditions of their tribe.

ASSEMBLY SONGS: TEXTS
FREE TRANSLATIONS, AND INTERPRETATIONS

The material contained in this section was obtained in Santiago late in May, 1948, from Mr. J. M. Collío Huaiquilaf,[11] and was rechecked with him about two months later. He wrote

creencias araucanas," Rev. folklore chileno, Ano III, Entrega 4 (1912), 171 and footnotes 1 and 2.

[10] Cf. Guevara, op. cit., p. 9.

[11] Mr. J. Martín Collío Huaiquilaf is not entirely unknown to North American anthropologists. He was in the United States after the close of the first World War, and he occasionally served as an informant to Dr. Speck and Dr. Hallowell at the University of Pennsylvania. He also conferred with Dr. Brand in Santiago in March, 1941, and Brand has published a trilingual text furnished by Collío. See D. D. Brand, op. cit., pp. 24, 36-52. See also A. I. Hallowell, "Araucanian Parallels to the Omaha Kinship Pattern," Amer. Anthropol., XLV (1943), 489-91.

Mr. Collío formerly lived on the reduccíon called Carrarriñe, near Cholchol, but for some years past he has been a resident of Santiago. He speaks Araucanian and Spanish fluently and has some knowledge of English. I found him to be a helpful and reliable informant, and I am deeply grateful for all the assistance he gave me.

ASSEMBLY SONGS

out the texts in his own hand, using a system of transcription that consists essentially of the values given to the Spanish alphabet, with the sole addition of a Germanic ü. Because of the metaphorical quality of the language, it was impossible to translate the texts literally, but the free translations given here were gone over word by word with Mr. Collío. The interpretations are, in all instances, based on data furnished by him, but I have supplied some additional material.

Mr. Collío unhesitatingly affirmed that the custom of singing at assemblies is still practiced throughout the Araucanian region. As a tribal leader he travels widely in central Chile, and he claims to have attended a great number of public gatherings at some of which he heard renditions of the songs given below. In Collío's home reservation, however, where I spent approximately six weeks, informants were not familiar with the texts of these songs. Apparently none of them has more than a local distribution in the vicinity in which it was composed.

Woman's Song No. 1[12]

kanin peuman
petu ñi ilchalen
ñi femguechi
niyer keael meu.

Free translation.—I dreamed of a vulture when I was a young virgin, little realizing that I was destined to submit to such a man.

Interpretation.—The singer complains that her husband is rapacious and inconsiderate. According to Collío, she is also implying that her spouse does not satisfy her sexual desires.

Man's Reply[13]

felelai papai
eimi palelai

---

[12] Women's songs are generally but not invariably shorter than are men's. The numbers attached to the successive texts are purely arbitrary and are used only for convenience in making references.

[13] There seems to be a tendency for singing to develop into a sort of contest, for many songs make accusations which are answered by the person concerned.

inche ta eimi
deuman piuke
fente ini ayufiel
kimwe laimi piyael
fei - ula doi ayueyu
felen meu feipien
eimi ta sakin domo.

Free translation.—It is not so, my dear papai (literally, "mother," but used as a courteous or affectionate term of direct address by any man speaking to a mature woman). No matter what you say, I'll never hurt your feelings. My heart beats (deuman, literally, "is self-made" or "manufactured") only for you. You don't know what you are saying, because I love you very much. You are my dearest woman.

Woman's Song No. 2

tregul peuman
kuifi meu kai
welu fele pulai
alka pülelen.

Free translation.—I dreamed of a lapwing[14] a long time ago, and now I am like a hen under the wing of a rooster.

Interpretation.—In explaining this song my informant said that it is of the type sung by a young wife to call attention to the fact that her husband is sexually overactive. On hearing such a complaint, her relatives and friends try to advise her spouse to moderate his marital behavior. Sometimes a group of elderly men will arrange to meet the husband in private, without the wife's knowledge, in order to give him the benefit of their experience. Among other things they may tell the husband not to seek sexual satisfaction daily and to abstain from intercourse for at least twelve hours after a meal.

---

[14] Fray Félix Jose dé Augusta (Diccionario araucano-español /Santiago, 1916/, II, 230) identifies the tregle bird as Vanellus chilensis, the Chilean lapwing. As Collío described it, however, it was somewhat reminiscent of the European cuckoo, in that he claimed it was noisy, frequented muddy places, and had no nest of its own, but laid eggs anywhere.

ASSEMBLY SONGS

Man's Reply

ñuke anai ñuke
ñochi müten kimei
mute dungulmi
ñillatu piuke nguea fun
piukeye niye eli
fele kayu müten
tayu poyen külen
inchiu meu ta
dungu kilpe che
inchiu müten kisu.

Free translation.—Wife, dear wife,[15] it would be better if you went more slowly and did not talk so much, or else there may be someone else asking for my favor (literally, piuke, "heart"). If you feel the same love for me that I do for you, just be quiet. Don't set people to talking about us; this is our own affair.

Woman's Counterreply

koñi anai koñi
müna küme küllüi
tami feipi fiel
ruf künu lan tatei.

Free translation.—Husband, dear husband,[16] what you have said shows that you just jumped at conclusions. I wasn't speaking seriously.

Interpretation.—It seems evident from the readings of the free translations in this group of three songs that a young wife sought to take advantage of Mapuche custom to draw attention to her husband's faults. When he called her to task in his reply, she tried to pass the matter off as a kind of joke.

---

[15] Traditionally, and to some extent at present, a Mapuche man was expected to marry the daughter of his mother's brother. The term for this cross-cousin is ñuke and may be used either in the literal sense of "wife" or else somewhat loosely to connote "sweetheart."

[16] A woman calls her husband koñi, the term for father's sister's son, because in former times she was expected to marry such a cross-cousin. Compare footnote 15.

Woman's Song No. 3

ngüru peuman
ni wesayauan meu
chum nguea afui
femguei feleael.

Free translation.—I dreamed of a fox. It was bad for me, but there is no help for it now, since that is the way it turned out to be.

Interpretation.—After having been married for two years or so, a wife has come to realize that her husband is like a fox, in the sense that he is given to thieving and wrongdoing.[17] Interested auditors, acting on this hint, make it a point to advise the husband to mend his ways. They also remind him that he has now been married long enough to realize that he ought to settle down and accept the responsibilities of a married man.

Man's Reply

müna wesa pimi
nai pichi nuke
femkefuli ofpe
fachi antü kimgue
eimi meu müten
puai ñi lelilen
wesa dungu afai.

Free translation.—Things are not as bad as you have said, my little cousin (wife). If I have done anything wrong, it's all over now. Only on you do my eyes gaze. Let everything bad be ended.

Interpretation.—The husband expresses remorse for his errors and promises to mend his ways at once and henceforth to keep his mind only on his wife.

---

[17]It is a Mapuche convention that a man whose faults are publicized in an assembly song must neither show anger nor seek to punish his wife. Nevertheless, an ominous tone runs through the husband's reply to Woman's Song No. 2; and the wife's counterreply is distinctly conciliatory.

ASSEMBLY SONGS

Woman's Counterreply

feula anai koñi
tami un meu
kimael ayüpen
fei-ula nay ñi piuke
femül mi kimei
rume ayüeyu ula.

Free translation.—Just now, dear cousin (husband), I have heard what I wanted to hear from your own lips. Now my heart is restored to its proper place. If you do what is right, I shall love you more than ever.

Woman's Song No. 4

cod-cod peuma
küme peuman
fei neu felen
ñi rumue küme füta.

Free translation.—I dreamed of a deer. It was a good omen, and that is why I find myself with my lovely husband.
Interpretation.—To dream of a deer is particularly auspicious. The deer is regarded as a gentle and good animal that never hurts anyone and never spoils or destroys anything. When a wife sings in this fashion, all the auditors congratulate the happy couple, who are in need neither of advice nor guidance.

Woman's Song No. 5[18]

rumel re ko peuman
famguechi ñi konpayam
ko engu pod fotra kei
fei neu dungu ka lei.

Free translation.—I always dreamed only of clear water. That is how I thought things were going to be, but water and

---

[18] This song and the next two were termed piñmal kaun ("ironic" or "sarcastic") by Collío. According to him, songs of this type comprise an important form of social control among the Mapuche. Sometimes, it is the only way in which conduct can be regulated. For example, a man who beats his wife may be induced to stop if people are sarcastic to him.

dirt make mud, and that is far from good.

Interpretation.—A wife sings in this vein to make it known that she is maltreated by her husband's family, with whom she has to live according to the custom of patrilocal unilocal residence. On hearing such a complaint people speak to the singer's parents-in-law, urging them to be more considerate of their daughter-in-law.

Woman's Song No. 6

weda lerkei puñmo
dungu allkutun
fotum müten mülei
domo nguerke lai.

Free translation.—Things are very bad with me. My father-in-law pays attention only to his son, while I am dismissed as if I were dead.

Interpretation.—Once again the strain put on a woman by the custom of patrilocal unilocal residence is brought out. A wife is a newcomer to her husband's household and is very much subject to her father-in-law throughout his lifetime.[19]

Woman's Song No. 7

weda peuman
trafia müten
ñi fillka duam
me peuman müten.

Free translation.—I had a bad dream just last night. On account of my brother-in-law (fillka) I dreamed of nothing but dung.

Interpretation.—This song expresses unhappiness because a woman's brother-in-law is about to marry. Through the workings of the custom of unilocal patrilocal residence his marriage means that another woman will come to live in the singer's household and will share in the conduct of its affairs. Women who are married to brothers often are so hostile that

---

[19] There is reason to believe that in former times a mature man maintained strong control over the inmates of his household. Normally, these consisted of his wives and unmarried offspring and his married sons and their wives and unwed children.

ASSEMBLY SONGS

they call each other <u>medomo</u> ("feces woman").[20]

When people hear a song of this kind, which is sung in the presence of the brother-in-law concerned, they keep it in mind but can take no action, since the marriage has not yet occurred. They note the hint of impending trouble, however, and prepare to serve as mediators and conciliators at the first sign of strife. Toward this end a secret committee of friendly and related women may be formed in order to establish amicable relations between the singer and her prospective sister-in-law.

Woman's Song No. 8

re kochü dungu
piyeninga welu
afkerkelu kochütun
fei ula fre letui
tami dungun
ellaka feipi feli.

<u>Free translation.</u>—At first you used to say only sweet things to me, but now the sweetness is gone and your speech is bitter. Please speak to me as you used to do in the beginning.

<u>Interpretation.</u>—Acting on the complaint expressed here, a group of responsible men may take it upon themselves to find out what has gone wrong and to take steps to bring about a reconciliation. Since Mapuche men talk more freely than do women about their private affairs, the group usually has some prior awareness of the husband's side of the case; but the wife's point of view may be entirely unknown up to this moment. As a matter of fact, Collío expressed the opinion that a woman would not sing in this way unless she had been long married and had acquired a feeling of security as the dominant female in her household.

Woman's Song No. 9

maicoño kuntrul
inaful inche meu
pün-pün külei

---

[20] Cf. De Augusta, <u>op. cit.</u>, I, 133.

inche püle müten
fenguechi peuman
tañi ñadu nguen meu.

Free translation.—A flock of turtledoves[21] flutters constantly by my side, wherever I may happen to be. In this way did I dream because of my nadu ("husband's sister").

Interpretation.—Although this type of song is called wenañkun ("sadness") it really expresses the opposite emotion. It reveals the good news that a woman's sister-in-law is about to be married. By the rule of patrilocal residence it follows that the singer is about to lose the companionship of her husband's sister, who was always fluttering about her. Deep down, the singer is pleased at the prospect of being left alone in her house with her husband and children.[22] Indeed, everyone may be said to be pleased: the prospective bride, her brother, her sister-in-law, and those of the bystanders who entertain hopes of taking part in the wedding celebration. Thus, this song "hurts no one," as Collío put it, and people hasten to wish joy to the girl whose betrothal the singer has announced. Just the same, Collío added, no woman would sing publicly in this manner, unless she were herself long-married and confident of her own security.

Man's Song No. 1[23]

kiñe ngue meu
ella lelien feichi
elu ad laen
rume kutrantun
tami fem fiel
re kura piuke
ütruf niyen.

Free translation.—Only with one eye do you glance at me at present. When you hide your face, I might as well be dead.

[21] De Augusta, op. cit., I, 128, identified maikoño as la tortola, the turtledove (Zenaida aurita).

[22] Contrast a wife's bitterness, in "Woman's Song No. 7," at the prospect of having a new sister-in-law move into her household.

[23] "Man's Songs" No. 1 and No. 2 were called dakeltun ül ("pact-making song") by Collío. As he used the term it had the connotation of a love pact.

Why must you ever show me nothing but a heart of stone?

Interpretation.—A boy sings in this fashion to his sweetheart, either during a family visit to her home or at an assembly where members of both families are present. It reveals the fact that he has failed to win the girl of his choice, and it also serves to test her reaction. In accordance with Mapuche conventions it is not proper for a young woman to accept a proposal too quickly or too directly. Hence, she answers in the manner of the reply given below. If the affair reaches a stalemate the suitor's father, confident of the singer's sincerity, may take steps leading to a formal betrothal.

Woman's Reply

müna koila wentru
piuke meu feipilai
re mellfu-un meu
müten feipi kei
angue ta pengue
küle kei müten
piuke ellka lei.

Free translation.—Men are all liars, they speak only with the lips, not with the heart. They show their faces uncovered, but not their hearts.

Interpretation.—By singing in such a vein, a girl who is being courted makes it clear that she is not to be taken lightly. The implication is that she may consider a serious offer of marriage but that she is unwilling to take part in a mere flirtation.

Man's Song No. 2

chumül anchi
inche kiman
tami piuke
ni inchü ngueael
feipi keeli
feichi dungu
allkutu anai
küme pichi ñuke.

Free translation.—When will the time come when I shall know what is in your heart? Why don't you say the word that will allow us to be united? Please listen to me, my little cousin.

Interpretation.—A lover will sing in this way if a sweetheart continues to show reluctance even after some of the preliminaries to marriage have been carried out. The intent is to persuade the girl to set a wedding date.

Woman's Reply

prolei ñi piuke
feipi keeli arol
piuke ta pekan
fam tuku keel
troki kifilngue
rulpa fingue
amulechi antu
fei ula kimaimin.

Free translation.—At this moment my heart is tied in a knot, so I cannot reply. The heart is not a toy to be lightly given away. Please do not hurry me. Let the ever-moving sun go on, then you will learn what is best.

Interpretation.—In these words a girl expresses her unwillingness to set a definite wedding date. Her song implies that she may yet be willing to marry her suitor, but is not interested in a casual love affair.

Man's Song No. 3[24]

inaltu mahuida
amulerpu fun
welu pela eyu ñuke
cheu anta mülei
tami piuke am
inche kutran piuke
eimi ayene-en
papai anai papai

---

[24] Strictly speaking this song is not rendered in public. It deals with a request for a private love affair and is addressed only to the girl concerned. Nevertheless, the lover may make his plea during the course of a large assembly.

chumül chefel
inche ta eimi chachai.

Free translation.—Along the edge of the forest I happened to go, but I failed to see you, cousin. Why are you so heartless?[25] While I am sick at heart, you are laughing at me. Mother, dear mother,[26] when will you say, "I am yours, daddy."[27]

Interpretation.—Here a lover complains that his sweetheart is not responsive to his advances. No serious offer of marriage is proposed, however.

Woman's Reply

koñi anai koñi
müfüchi ñuke
rume piyaimi
welu rüpü kilñe
kiso lelmi rume
feipi afeyu
trig mapu meu
wefpalen inche
pu che meu ta tripan.

Free translation.—Cousin, dear cousin, no matter how often you may call me ñuke ("cousin" or "wife"),[28] you are on the wrong road. Let me remind you that I did not spring from a hole in the ground, but was born from a human body.

Interpretation.—In this song a young woman expresses her refusal to engage in an irregular love affair with her father's sister's son. Because this type of cross-cousin marriage was the Mapuche pattern, young men were apt to regard all of their ñuke (mother's brother's daughters) as potential mistresses, if not wives. Parents were, of course, fully cognizant of this attitude and took pains, accordingly, to warn their eligible

[25] Tami piuke am means literally, "your heart soul." However, am also means "shade" or "reflection." Thus, the lover wants to know where is the soul, shade, or reflection of his cousin's heart. This connotes that she appears heartless to him.

[26] For the use of papai see the free translation of "Man's Reply" to "Woman's Song No. 1."

[27] Chachai is a familiar term for father. It may also be used as a friendly greeting by a young woman addressing an older man.

[28] Compare footnote 15.

daughters not to yield too readily to their importunate cousins.

CONCLUSION

The songs contained in the preceding section represent only a part of the repertoire of a single, well-versed informant. No doubt vast stores of similar material await systematic collection. Unquestionably, too, they will yield many insights into the workings of Mapuche culture and its effects on the temperaments of the people.

For women, especially, the device of assembly singing seems to afford an important emotional outlet. Traditionally, Araucanian social organization has a strong masculine emphasis, and women have only minor and subordinate status.[29] This is particularly apparent in the marriage customs, for women have scarcely any voice in the selection of mates, they have nothing to say about where they are going to live, and they have little expectation of being sole mistresses of their own households. That these matters trouble them is clearly evident from the way in which wives take advantage of a socially approved safety valve that gives them an opportunity to "blow off steam" regarding their marital problems, without fear of criticism or reprisals.

It is the postmarital residence pattern that appears to put the greatest strain on a newlywed woman. While a groom continues to live on his natal reducción, sometimes in the very house in which he was born, a bride must go to live among strangers in a strange place. Not only must she work out an adjustment to her husband but also to such of his relatives as happen to live under the same roof. Some of the personality clashes that are likely to grow out of this situation are revealed in "Woman's Song" Nos. 5, 6, 7, and 9.

Another aspect of Mapuche social organization that finds recurrent expression in the songs is the emphasis on cross-cousin marriage. So close is the bond between a man and his mother's brother's daughter (koñi-ñuke) that one may use the term ñuke for a wife or sweetheart who is not a daughter of one's maternal uncle.

---

[29] The fact that most of the religious leaders (machis) are women makes an important exception to the general rule.

CONCLUSION

The assembly songs also serve to call attention to several items of Mapuche religion. Belief in dreams as omens is frequently reiterated, and there is one interesting example of the widely held notion that heart, soul, shade, and reflection form a single complex. Furthermore, there are some references to bird and animal lore, with mention being made specifically of the deer, fox, vulture, lapwing, turtledove, hen, and rooster.

In conclusion, it may be said that these songs give proof of the high poetic quality of Mapuche oral literature. At the same time they throw light on numerous aspects of social organization and provide important clues to an understanding of the interplay between Mapuche culture and personality development.

www.ingramcontent.com/pod-product-compliance
Lightning Source LLC
Jackson TN
JSHW070314120426
100741JS00007B/61